·Cooking for Today·

VEGETARIAN THAI COOKING

·*Cooking for Today*·

VEGETARIAN THAI COOKING

CARA HOBDAY

SMITHMARK

Distributed in the USA by SMITHMARK Publishers,
a division of U.S. Media Holdings Inc.,
16, East 32nd Street, New York, NY 10016

Copyright © 1995 Parragon Book Service Ltd, Bristol, England

SMITHMARK books are available for bulk purchase for sales promotion and premium use.
For details, write or call the Manager of Special Sales, SMITHMARK publishers,
16 East 32nd Street, New York, NY 10016; (212) 532-6600

ISBN 0-7651-9862-2

10 9 8 7 6 5 4 3 2 1

Produced by Haldane Mason, London

Printed in Italy

Acknowledgements:
Art Direction: Ron Samuels
Editor: Joanna Swinnerton
Series Design: Pedro & Frances Prá-Lopez / Kingfisher Design
Page Design: F14 Creative Consultants
Photography and styling: Sue Atkinson
Home Economist: Cara Hobday

Photographs on pages 6, 20, 34, 46, 62 reproduced by permission of ZEFA Picture Library (UK) Ltd.
The photographer would like to thank Dynasty Oriental Emporium, Windsor, for the
loan of equipment.

Note:
*Cup measurements in this book are for American cups. Tablespoons are assumed to be 15ml. Unless otherwise
stated, milk is assumed to be full-fat, eggs are AA extra large and pepper is freshly ground black pepper.*

Contents

❧

CHAPTER ONE

Soups & Appetizers

Food and hospitality are an important part of daily life in the countries of South-east Asia. In Thailand, the traditional way to share the pleasures of eating together is to sit down with your family and friends to a meal that is served as one course of many different dishes. Usually a fried dish, a steamed or stewed dish, and a curry are arranged around a communal bowl of steaming, fluffy, fragrant rice, and a bowl of soup is served alongside.

Although there is usually no first course in traditional Thai meals, one may often find that smaller dishes are served before the main course in restaurants in Thailand that cater for foreigners and tourists, or in Thai restaurants in other countries where a light appetizer is usual. It is pleasant to have an appetizer as a prelude to the meal to follow, and there are many dishes in the Thai cuisine that make excellent appetizers.

Opposite: *An extraordinary rock formation graces the shores of Phuket in southern Thailand.*

STEP 1

STEP 2

STEP 3

STEP 3

HOT & SOUR SOUP

A very traditional staple of the Thai national diet, this soup is sold on street corners, at food bars, and by mobile vendors all over the country.

SERVES 4

1 tbsp sunflower oil
8 ounces smoked tofu, sliced
1 cup shiitake mushrooms, sliced
2 tbsp chopped fresh cilantro
2 cups watercress
1 red chili, finely sliced, to garnish

STOCK:
1 tbsp tamarind pulp
2 dried red chilies, chopped
2 kaffir lime leaves, torn in half
1-in. piece ginger, chopped
2-in. piece galangal, chopped
1 stalk lemon grass, chopped
1 onion, quartered
4 cups cold water

1 Put all the ingredients for the stock into a saucepan, and bring to a boil. Simmer for 5 minutes. Remove from the heat, and strain, reserving the stock.

2 Heat the oil in a wok, and cook the tofu over a high heat for about 2 minutes, stirring constantly. Add the strained stock.

3 Add the mushrooms and cilantro, and boil for 3 minutes. Add the watercress, and boil for 1 minute.

4 Serve immediately, garnished with red chili slices.

MUSHROOMS

You may like to try a mixture of different types of mushroom. Oyster, button, and straw mushrooms are all suitable.

8

STEP 1

STEP 3

STEP 4

STEP 5

NOODLE, MUSHROOM, & GINGER SOUP

Thai soups are very quickly and easily put together, and are cooked so that each ingredient can still be tasted even after it has been combined with several others.

SERVES 4

$\frac{1}{4}$ *cup dried Chinese mushrooms or 1$\frac{1}{3}$ cups field or crimini mushrooms*
4 cups hot vegetable stock
4 ounces thread egg noodles
2 tsp sunflower oil
3 garlic cloves, crushed
1-in. piece ginger, finely shredded
$\frac{1}{2}$ *tsp mushroom ketchup*
1 tsp light soy sauce
2 cups bean-sprouts
cilantro leaves to garnish

1 Soak the dried Chinese mushrooms, if using, for at least 30 minutes in 1$\frac{1}{4}$ cups of the hot vegetable stock. Remove the stalks and discard, then slice the mushrooms. Reserve the stock.

2 Cook the noodles for 2–3 minutes in boiling water. Drain and rinse. Set them aside.

3 Heat the oil over a high heat in a wok or large, heavy skillet. Add the garlic and ginger, and stir. Add the mushrooms, and stir over a high heat for 2 minutes.

4 Add the remaining vegetable stock with the reserved stock, and bring to a boil. Add the mushroom ketchup and soy sauce.

5 Stir in the bean-sprouts. Cook until tender, and then serve immediately over the noodles, garnished with the cilantro leaves.

DRIED CHINESE MUSHROOMS

Dried Chinese mushrooms are widely available from all oriental stores and markets. They are quite inexpensive, and will keep for an extended period in a sealed jar.

FILLED CUCUMBER CUPS

There are two types of Thai cooking: the elaborate Royal cooking, and the peasant style of cooking. This dish is from the Royal cuisine, where care is taken over presentation, and the flavors are subtle.

STEP 1

SERVES 6

1 English cucumber
4 scallions, finely chopped
4 tbsp lime juice
2 small red chilies, deseeded and finely chopped
3 tsp sugar
1¼ cups ground roasted peanuts
¼ tsp salt
3 shallots, finely sliced and deep-fried to garnish

1 To make the cucumber cups, cut the ends off the cucumber, and divide it into 3 equal lengths. Mark a line around the center of each one as a guide.

2 Make a zigzag cut all the way around the center of each section, always pointing the knife toward the center of the cucumber. Pull apart the two halves.

3 Scoop out the center of each cucumber cup with a melon baller or teaspoon.

4 Put the remaining ingredients, except for the shallots, in a bowl, and mix well to combine.

5 Divide the filling between the 6 cups, and arrange on a serving plate. Garnish with the deep-fried shallots.

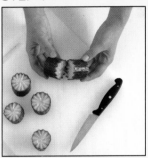

STEP 2

CHERRY TOMATOES

Cherry tomatoes can also be hollowed out very simply with a melon baller and filled with this mixture. The two look very pretty arranged together on a serving dish.

STEP 4

STEP 5

STEP 1

STEP 2

STEP 3

STEP 5

RICE CUBES WITH DIPPING SAUCE

Plain rice cubes are a good foil to any piquant dipping sauce, and they are often served with satay, to complement the dipping sauce.

SERVES 4–6

1½ cups Thai jasmine rice
5 cups water

CILANTRO DIPPING SAUCE:
1 garlic clove
2 tsp salt
1 tbsp black peppercorns
1 cup washed cilantro, including roots and
* stem*
3 tbsp lemon juice
¾ cup coconut milk
2 tbsp peanut butter
2 scallions, roughly chopped
1 red chili, deseeded and sliced

1 Grease and line an 8 × 4 × 1 in. pan. A brownie pan is ideal.

2 To make the sauce, put the garlic, salt, peppercorns, cilantro, and lemon juice into a pestle and mortar or blender. Grind finely.

3 Add the coconut milk, peanut butter, scallions, and chili. Grind finely. Transfer to a saucepan, and bring to a boil. Let cool. This sauce will keep for 3–5 days in a refrigerator.

4 To cook the rice, do not rinse. Bring the water to a boil, and add the rice. Stir and return to a medium boil. Cook, uncovered, for 14 –16 minutes until very soft. Drain thoroughly.

5 Put ⅔ cup of the cooked rice in a blender and purée, or grind to a paste in a pestle and mortar. Stir into the remaining cooked rice, and spoon into the lined pan. Level the surface and cover with plastic wrap. Compress the rice by using either a similar-sized pan which will fit into the filled pan, or a small piece of board, and weigh this down with cans. Chill for at least 8 hours or preferably overnight.

6 Invert the pan onto a board. Cut the rice into cubes with a wet knife. Serve with the Cilantro Dipping Sauce.

RICE

This recipe would work equally well with Basmati rice, but avoid using any rice labelled "easy cook" or "par-boiled" as you will have disappointing results.

STEP 1

STEP 2

STEP 3

STEP 5

FRIED TOFU WITH PEANUT SAUCE

This is a very sociable dish, if put in the center of the table where people can help themselves with toothpicks.

SERVES 4

1 pound tofu, marinated or plain
2 tbsp rice vinegar
2 tbsp sugar
1 tsp salt
3 tbsp smooth peanut butter
$^1/_2$ tsp chili flakes
3 tbsp barbecue sauce
4 cups sunflower oil
2 tbsp sesame oil

BATTER:
4 tbsp all-purpose flour
2 eggs, beaten
4 tbsp milk
$^1/_2$ tsp baking powder
$^1/_2$ tsp chili powder

1 Cut the tofu into 1 in. triangles. Set aside.

2 Combine the vinegar, sugar, and salt in a saucepan. Bring to a boil and then simmer for 2 minutes. Remove from the heat, and add the peanut butter, chili flakes, and barbecue sauce.

3 To make the batter, sift the flour into a bowl, and make a well in the center. Add the eggs, and draw in the flour, adding the milk slowly. Stir in the baking powder and chili powder.

4 Heat both the oils in a deep-fryer or large saucepan until a light haze appears on top.

5 Dip the tofu triangles into the batter and deep-fry until golden-brown. Drain on paper towels.

6 Serve with the peanut sauce.

FRYING TOFU

You may find it easier to pick up the tofu triangles on a fork or skewer in order to coat them in batter before placing them in the hot oil.

STEP 1

STEP 2

STEP 3

STEP 4

EGGPLANT DIPPING SAUCE PLATTER

Dipping platters are a very sociable dish, bringing the whole table together. I like to serve a substantial dip with vegetables as an appetizer.

SERVES 4

1 eggplant, peeled and cut into 1 in.
  cubes
3 tbsp sesame seeds, roasted in a dry pan
  over a low heat
1 tsp sesame oil
grated rind and juice of ¹/₂ lime
1 small shallot, diced
¹/₂ tsp salt
1 tsp sugar
1 red chili, deseeded and sliced
1¹/₄ cups broccoli florets
2 carrots, cut into matchsticks
8 baby corn, cut in half lengthwise
2 celery stalks, cut into matchsticks
1 baby red cabbage, cut into 8 wedges, each
  wedge held together by the core

1 Cook the diced eggplant in boiling water for 7–8 minutes.

2 Meanwhile, grind the sesame seeds with the oil in a food processor or pestle and mortar.

3 Add the eggplant, lime rind and juice, shallot, salt, sugar, and chili in that order, to the sesame.

4 Process, or chop and mash by hand, until smooth. Taste for seasoning before spooning into a bowl. Serve surrounded by the broccoli, carrots, baby corn, celery, and red cabbage.

SALTING EGGPLANTS

I never salt the eggplant unless it is particularly large and likely to be bitter. The Thais never salt eggplants as theirs are so fresh and tender.

18

CHAPTER TWO

Rice & Noodles

The Thai signal that the meal is ready is *Kin khao* – literally translated this means "eat rice." Thai jasmine rice is the central part of the Thai diet, and every meal is based around it. Thais are in the habit of eating rice, and will eat at one sitting about twice as much as the average Westerner would, so naturally they are exacting about the quality of their rice, the taste, fragrance, and whiteness of it, and will pay for these points in a superior rice.

Nearly all modern Thai women possess at least two rice cookers each, and would be lost if asked to cook rice in a Western kitchen. Unlike our rice cookers, the Asian version is a sophisticated piece of equipment. But for the Western cook without a fancy rice cooker the absorption method is best, though there are two important things to remember: do not stir too much while the rice is cooking, as this will release the starch in the rice and make it stick together; and if you plan to reuse the rice, cool it down quickly by spreading it out on a tray and chilling it. When reheating, ensure that it is hot through, and reheat it only once.

Noodles are eaten at any time of the day or night in Thailand, as a fast food prepared by numerous roadside vendors, who will whip up, before your very eyes, a tasty and spicy noodle dish to see you through to the next food stop, which will not be very far away.

Opposite: *A moat temple in Chiang Mai presents a peaceful scene.*

METHOD 1: STEP 1

METHOD 1: STEP 2

METHOD 2: STEP 2

METHOD 2: STEP 3

THAI JASMINE RICE

Every Thai meal has as its centerpiece a big bowl of steaming, fluffy Thai jasmine rice. The method used for cooking rice in Thailand is the absorption method, but I have also given below the open pan method, as this is the one most familiar to Western cooks. Salt should not be added.

SERVES 3–4

1. OPEN PAN METHOD

generous 1 cup Thai jasmine rice
4 cups water

1 Rinse the uncooked rice in a strainer under cold running water, and let drain.

2 Bring the water to a boil. Add the rice, and stir. Return to a medium boil, and cook, uncovered, for 8–10 minutes.

3 Drain and fork through lightly before serving.

2. ABSORPTION METHOD

generous 1 cup Thai jasmine rice
scant 2 cups water

1 Rinse the rice in a strainer under cold running water.

2 Put the rice and water into a saucepan, and bring to a boil. Stir once, and then cover the pan tightly. Lower the heat as much as possible. Cook for 10 minutes. Let rest for 5 minutes.

3 Fork through lightly, and serve immediately.

MICROWAVING AND FREEZING

Thai jasmine rice can also be cooked in a microwave oven. Use generous 1 cup rice to scant 2 cups boiling water. Combine in a bowl. Cover and cook on High for 5 minutes. Stir, cover, and cook on Defrost for 6 minutes. Let sit for 3 minutes. Fork through lightly, and serve. Freeze in a plastic sealed container. Frozen rice is ideal for stir-fry dishes, as the process seems to separate the grains.

STEP 1

STEP 2

STEP 4

STEP 4

GREEN RICE

*A deliciously different way to serve plain rice
for a special occasion or simply to liven up
a simple meal.*

SERVES 4

2 tbsp olive oil
2¼ cups Basmati or Thai jasmine rice,
   soaked for 1 hour, washed and
   drained
3 cups coconut milk
1 tsp salt
1 bay leaf
2 tbsp chopped fresh cilantro
2 tbsp chopped fresh mint
2 green chilies, deseeded and finely
   chopped

1 Heat the oil in a saucepan. Add the rice, and stir until the grains are translucent.

2 Add the coconut milk, salt, and bay leaf. Bring to a boil, and cook until all the liquid is absorbed.

3 Lower the heat as much as possible. Cover the saucepan tightly, and cook for 10 minutes.

4 Remove the bay leaf, and stir in the cilantro, mint, and green chilies. Fork through the rice gently, and serve.

GARNISHES

The contrasting colors of this dish make it particularly attractive, and it can be made to look even more interesting with a carefully chosen garnish. Two segments of fresh lime complement the green cilantro perfectly. Alternatively, you could simply use some small sprigs of whole fresh cilantro leaves.

COOKING IN THE MICROWAVE

To save time, or to make some space on your stove, step 3 can also be done in a microwave. Transfer the rice to a microwave container, cover tightly, and cook on High for 4–5 minutes. Remove the bay leaf, and stir in the herbs and chilies. Fork through the rice gently, and serve.

STEP 1

STEP 2

STEP 3

STEP 3

CHATUCHAK FRIED RICE

An excellent way to use up leftover rice! Pop it in the freezer as soon as it is cool. It will be ready to use at any time, and the freezing seems to separate the grains beautifully. This dish should be reheated only once.

SERVES 4

1 tbsp sunflower oil
3 shallots, finely chopped
2 garlic cloves, crushed
1 red chili, deseeded and finely chopped
1-in. piece ginger, finely shredded
1/2 green bell pepper, deseeded and finely sliced
2–3 baby eggplants, quartered
3 ounces sugar snap peas, trimmed and
    blanched
6 baby corn, halved lengthwise
    and blanched
1 tomato, cut into 8 pieces
1 1/2 cups bean-sprouts
3 cups cooked Thai jasmine rice (see
    page 22)
2 tbsp tomato ketchup
2 tbsp light soy sauce

TO GARNISH:
cilantro leaves
lime wedges

1 Heat the oil in a wok or large, heavy skillet over a high heat. Add the chopped shallots, garlic, chili, and ginger. Stir until the shallots have softened.

2 Add the green bell pepper and baby eggplants, and stir. Add the sugar snap peas, baby corn, tomato, and bean-sprouts. Stir for 3 minutes.

3 Add the rice, and lift and stir with 2 spoons for 4–5 minutes, until no more steam is released. Stir in the tomato ketchup and soy sauce.

4 Serve immediately, garnished with cilantro leaves and lime wedges to squeeze over.

VARIATION

Almost any vegetable, such as celery, eggplant, water chestnuts, bamboo shoots, carrots, beans, cauliflower, or broccoli can be used. Harder vegetables may need blanching to equalize the cooking time.

THAI-STYLE STIR-FRIED NOODLES

This dish is considered the Thai national dish, as it is made everywhere, a favorite fast food, one-dish meal for Thais on the go.

STEP 1

SERVES 4

8 ounces dried rice noodles
2 red chilies, deseeded and finely chopped
2 shallots, finely chopped
2 tbsp sugar
2 tbsp tamarind water
1 tbsp lime juice
2 tbsp light soy sauce
black pepper
1 tbsp sunflower oil
1 tsp sesame oil
¾ cup diced smoked tofu
2 tbsp chopped roasted peanuts

1 Cook the rice noodles as directed on the package, or soak them in boiling water for 5 minutes.

2 Grind together the chilies, shallots, sugar, tamarind water, lime juice, light soy sauce, and black pepper.

3 Heat both the oils together in a wok or large, heavy skillet over a high heat. Add the tofu, and stir for 1 minute.

4 Add the chili mixture. Bring to a boil, and stir for about 2 minutes until thickened.

5 Drain the rice noodles and add them to the chili mixture. Using 2 spoons, lift and stir them until they are no longer steaming. Serve immediately, garnished with the peanuts.

STEP 2

STEP 4

ONE-DISH MEAL

This is a very quick one-dish meal if you are catering for a single vegetarian in the family.

STEP 5

STEP 1

STEP 2

STEP 3

STEP 4

CRISPY DEEP-FRIED NOODLES

This is the staple dish on every Thai restaurant menu by which the establishment will be judged. It does require a certain amount of care and attention to get the crispy noodles properly cooked.

SERVES 4

6 ounces thread egg noodles
2$\frac{1}{2}$ cups sunflower oil for deep-frying
2 tsp grated lemon peel
1 tbsp light soy sauce
1 tbsp rice vinegar
1 tbsp lemon juice
1$\frac{1}{2}$ tbsp sugar
1 cup diced marinated tofu
2 garlic cloves, crushed
1 red chili, deseeded and finely sliced
1 red bell pepper, deseeded and diced
4 eggs, beaten
red chili, sliced, to garnish

1 Blanch the egg noodles briefly in hot water, to which a little of the oil has been added. Drain and spread out to dry for at least 30 minutes. Cut into threads about 3 inches long.

2 Combine the lemon peel, light soy sauce, rice vinegar, lemon juice, and sugar in a small bowl.

3 Heat the oil in a wok or large, heavy skillet, and test the temperature with a few strands of noodles. They should swell to many times their size, but if they do not, wait until the oil is hot enough; otherwise

they will be tough and stringy, not puffy and light. Cook them in batches. As soon as they turn a pale gold color, scoop them out, and drain on plenty of paper towels. Let cool.

4 Reserve 2 tbsp of the oil, and drain off the rest. Heat the 2 tbsp of oil in the wok or skillet. Cook the tofu quickly over a high heat to seal. Add the garlic, chili, and diced bell pepper. Stir for 1–2 minutes. Add the vinegar mixture to the pan, and stir. Add the eggs, stirring until they are set.

5 Serve with the crispy fried noodles, garnished with sliced red chili.

PERFECT NOODLES

For best results with this dish, the oil must be hot enough, and the noodles must be drained on paper towels immediately.

STEP 1

STEP 2

STEP 3

STEP 4

FRIED NOODLES WITH BEAN-SPROUTS, CHIVES, & CHILI

This is a simple idea to jazz up noodles which accompany main course dishes in Thailand.

SERVES 4

1 pound medium egg noodles
1 cup bean-sprouts
small bunch chives
3 tbsp sunflower oil
1 garlic clove, crushed
4 green chilies, deseeded, sliced, and soaked
   in 2 tbsp rice vinegar
salt

1 To cook the noodles, soak in boiling water for 10 minutes. Drain and set aside.

2 Soak the bean-sprouts in cold water, while you cut the chives into 1-in. pieces. Set a few chives aside for garnish. Drain the bean-sprouts thoroughly.

3 Heat the oil in a wok or large, heavy skillet. Add the crushed garlic and stir; then add the chilies, and stir until fragrant, about 1 minute.

4 Add the bean-sprouts, stir, and then add the noodles. Stir in some salt and the chives. Using 2 spoons, lift and stir the noodles for 1 minute.

5 Garnish the finished dish with the reserved chives, and serve immediately.

CHILIES

Soaking a chili in rice vinegar has the effect of distributing the hot chili flavor throughout the dish. To reduce the heat, you can slice the chili more thickly before soaking, or soak it once in vinegar or hot water, discard the soaking liquid, then soak the chili again in a fresh batch of rice vinegar before adding the vinegar and chili to the dish.

HERBS

A variety of fresh herbs can be stirred through rice and noodles to make them a little special. Cilantro and mint are also a very successful combination.

CHAPTER THREE

Main Course Dishes

Thai cookery is based on a very different set of rules, methods, and techniques from those by which we cook in the West. Thai cooks often have to work with only what is available; this, combined with the various simple cooking methods of stir-frying, steaming, and deep-frying, means that the cuisine is wide open to interpretation. One dish can have four different tastes in four different regions, and the variety of dishes is as infinite as the number of cooks.

People's tastes and kitchens vary widely in other countries too, so do not be afraid to adapt and experiment with these recipes. For instance, you could try substituting another firm vegetable in the Eggplant and Mushroom Satay with Peanut Sauce (see page 42), or extending the Massaman Curried Rice (see page 41) with extra vegetables. Adapt the recipes to your personal preference and to the fresh produce available – and do not forget the Thai spirit of *Sanuk* – fun!

Opposite: *Temple ruins of Ayutthaya.*

STEP 1

STEP 2

STEP 3

STEP 4

RED CURRY WITH CASHEWS

This is a wonderfully quick dish to prepare. The paste can be bought ready-prepared and is very satisfactory, but it has a delicious aroma when homemade. It will keep for up to 3 weeks in the refrigerator.

SERVES 4

3 tbsp Red Curry Paste
1 cup coconut milk
1 kaffir lime leaf, mid-rib removed
$^{1}/_{4}$ tsp light soy sauce
4 baby corn, halved lengthwise
$1^{1}/_{4}$ cups broccoli florets
4 ounces green beans, cut into 2-in.
    pieces
$^{1}/_{4}$ cup cashew nuts
15 fresh basil leaves
1 tbsp chopped fresh cilantro
1 tbsp chopped roast peanuts to garnish

RED CURRY PASTE
7 fresh red chilies, halved, deseeded, and
    blanched (use dried if fresh are not
    available)
2 tsp cumin seeds
2 tsp coriander seeds
1-in. piece galangal, peeled and chopped
$^{1}/_{2}$ stalk lemon grass, chopped
1 tsp salt
grated rind of 1 lime
4 garlic cloves, chopped
3 shallots, chopped
2 kaffir lime leaves, mid-rib removed,
    shredded
1 tbsp oil to blend

1 To make the curry paste, grind all the ingredients together in a large pestle and mortar, food processor, or grinder. The paste will keep for up to 3 weeks in a sealed jar in the refrigerator.

2 Put a wok or large, heavy skillet over a high heat. Add the red curry paste, and stir until fragrant. Reduce the heat.

3 Add the coconut milk, lime leaf, light soy sauce, baby corn, broccoli, beans, and cashew nuts. Bring to a boil, and simmer for about 10 minutes until the vegetables are cooked, but still firm.

4 Remove the lime leaf, and stir in the basil leaves and cilantro. Serve over rice, garnished with peanuts.

VARIATION

Thai shops often have small, green, pea eggplants which have a very peppery taste, and are excellent when cooked in this dish. They can be quite firm, and should be blanched before adding to the curry with the other vegetables.

STEP 1

STEP 3

STEP 4

STEP 5

GREEN CURRY WITH TEMPEH

There are three basic curries in Thai cuisine, of which the green curry is the hottest, red curry is medium, and Massaman curry is the mildest. The green curry paste will keep for up to 3 weeks in the refrigerator. Serve over rice and noodles.

SERVES 4

1 tbsp sunflower oil
6 ounces marinated or plain tempeh, cut into
    diamonds (see page 79)
6 scallions, cut into 1-in. pieces
²/₃ cup coconut milk
6 tbsp Green Curry Paste, either bought or
    prepared
grated rind of 1 lime
¹/₄ cup fresh basil leaves
¹/₄ tsp liquid seasoning, such as Maggi

GREEN CURRY PASTE:
2 tsp coriander seeds
1 tsp cumin seeds
1 tsp black peppercorns
4 large green chilies, deseeded
2 shallots, quartered
2 garlic cloves, peeled
2 tbsp chopped fresh cilantro, including root
    and stalk
grated rind of 1 lime
1 tbsp roughly chopped galangal
1 tsp ground turmeric
salt
2 tbsp oil

TO GARNISH:
fresh cilantro leaves
2 green chilies, thinly sliced

1 To make the green curry paste, grind the coriander and cumin seeds and the peppercorns in a mortar and pestle or food processor.

2 Blend the remaining ingredients together and add the ground spice mixture. Store in a clean, dry jar for up to 3 weeks in the refrigerator, or freeze in a suitable container. Makes 6 tbsp.

3 Heat the oil in a wok or large, heavy skillet. Add the tempeh slices, and stir over a high heat for about 2 minutes, until sealed on all sides. Add the scallions, and cook, stirring, for 1 minute. Remove the tempeh and scallions, and reserve.

4 Put half the coconut milk into the wok or skillet and bring to a boil. Add the curry paste and lime rind, and cook until fragrant, about 1 minute. Add the reserved scallions, and tempeh.

5 Add the remaining coconut milk, and simmer for 7–8 minutes. Stir in the basil leaves and liquid seasoning. Simmer for one more minute before serving, garnished with cilantro leaves and chilies.

MASSAMAN CURRIED RICE

*Massaman paste is the mildest of Thai curry pastes, and owes its strong
aroma to its Muslim origins. This makes a deliciously rich curry.*

STEP 1

SERVES 4

PASTE:
1 tsp coriander seeds
1 tsp cumin seeds
1 tsp ground cinnamon
1 tsp cloves
1 whole star anise
1 tsp cardamom pods
1 tsp white peppercorns
1 tbsp oil
6 shallots, very roughly chopped
6 garlic cloves, very roughly chopped
2-in. piece lemon grass, sliced
4 fresh red chilies, deseeded and chopped
grated rind of 1 lime
1 tsp salt
1 tbsp chopped roast peanuts to garnish

CURRY:
3 tbsp sunflower oil
8 ounces marinated tofu, cut into 1-in. cubes
4 ounces green beans, cut into 1-in. lengths
6 cups cooked rice (1½ cups raw weight)
3 shallots, finely diced and deep-fried
1 scallion, finely chopped
2 tbsp chopped roast peanuts
1 tbsp lime juice

1 First, make the paste. Grind
together the seeds and spices in a
pestle and mortar or spice grinder.

2 Heat the oil in a saucepan or wok,
and add the shallots, garlic, and
lemon grass. Cook over a low heat until
soft, about 5 minutes. Then add the chili,
and grind together with the dry spices.
Stir in the lime rind and salt.

3 To make the curry, heat the oil in a
wok or large, heavy skillet. Cook
the tofu over a high heat for 2 minutes to
seal. Add the curry paste and beans, and
stir. Add the rice, and, using 2 spoons,
lift and stir over a high heat for about
3 minutes.

4 Transfer to a warmed serving dish.
Sprinkle with the deep-fried
shallots, scallion, and peanuts. Squeeze
over the lime juice.

STEP 2

STEP 3

VARIATION

A variety of crunchy vegetables can be
used in this dish. Celery, red bell peppers,
broccoli, snow peas, or shredded white
cabbage can all be used very successfully.

STEP 3

STEP 1

STEP 2

STEP 3

STEP 5

EGGPLANT & MUSHROOM SATAY WITH PEANUT SAUCE

Grilled, skewered vegetables are served with a satay sauce.

SERVES 4
8 wooden or metal skewers.
2 eggplants, cut into 1-in. pieces
6 ounces small crimini mushrooms

MARINADE:
1 tsp cumin seed
1 tsp coriander seed
1-in. piece ginger, grated
2 garlic cloves, lightly crushed
½ stalk lemon grass, roughly chopped
4 tbsp light soy sauce
8 tbsp sunflower oil
2 tbsp lemon juice

PEANUT SAUCE:
½ tsp cumin seed
½ tsp coriander seed
3 garlic cloves
1 small onion, quartered
1 tbsp lemon juice
1 tsp salt
½ red chili, deseeded and sliced
½ cup coconut milk
1 cup crunchy peanut butter
1 cup water

1 If using wooden skewers, soak in hand-hot water for 5 minutes. Thread the eggplant and mushroom onto the skewers, alternating the pieces.

2 To make the marinade, grind the cumin and coriander seeds, ginger, garlic, and lemon grass together. Put in a wok or a large, heavy skillet. Stir over a high heat until fragrant. Remove from the heat, and add the remaining marinade ingredients.

3 Place the skewers in a non-porous dish and spoon the marinade over them. Let marinate for a minimum of 2 hours and up to 8 hours.

4 To make the peanut sauce, grind together the cumin and coriander seeds and the garlic. Switch on your food processor or blender, and feed in the onion, or chop the onion finely by hand, then add to the cumin seed mixture. Add the remaining ingredients in order, except the water.

5 Transfer to a saucepan, and blend in the water. Bring to a boil and cook until the required thickness is reached. Transfer to a serving bowl.

6 Place the skewers on a baking sheet and cook under a preheated very hot broiler for 15–20 minutes. Brush with the marinade frequently and turn once. Serve hot with the peanut sauce.

STEP 1

STEP 2

STEP 2

STEP 3

THREE MUSHROOMS IN COCONUT MILK

A filling and tasty main course dish served over rice or noodles.

SERVES 4

2 lemon grass stalks, thinly sliced
2 green chilies, deseeded and finely chopped
1 tbsp light soy sauce
2 garlic cloves, crushed
2 tbsp chopped fresh cilantro
2 tbsp chopped fresh parsley
6 slices galangal, peeled
3 tbsp sunflower oil
1 eggplant, cubed
2/3 cup oyster mushrooms
2/3 cup crimini mushrooms
2/3 cup field mushrooms, quartered if large
4 ounces green beans, cut into 2-in. lengths,
    blanched
1 1/4 cups coconut milk
1 tbsp lemon juice
2 tbsp chopped roasted peanuts to garnish

1 Grind together the lemon grass, chilies, soy sauce, garlic, cilantro, parsley, and galangal in a large pestle and mortar or a food processor. Set aside.

2 Heat the sunflower oil in a wok or large, heavy skillet. Add the eggplant, and stir over a high heat for 3 minutes; then add the mushrooms, stir, and add the beans. Cook for 3 minutes, stirring constantly. Add the ground spice paste.

3 Add the coconut milk and lemon juice to the pan. Bring to the boil, and simmer for 2 minutes.

4 Serve immediately over rice, and garnish with the roasted peanuts.

VARIATION

Any mixture of tasty mushrooms can be used in this recipe. If using dried mushrooms, use 1 tbsp for every 2/3 cup fresh mushrooms.

CHAPTER FOUR

Vegetables

The recipes in this chapter are intended either as accompaniments for the main course dishes, or they can be served as versatile starters, buffet dishes, and light snacks. I have tried to keep the dishes light and delicate as a complement to the richer textures and more complex flavors of the main course dishes.

An astonishing variety of vegetables are found in the markets of Thailand. Most of these vegetables can now be found in your local supermarket or an oriental store. What you may not be able to obtain are the many varieties of eggplant found in Thailand in every size, shape, and color – they have the appearance of peas, the color of jewels, and the shape of cucumbers. Walking around a Thai market is a revelation to every foreign visitor; the infinite variety of fresh raw produce looks spectacular piled high. But there are many delicious and authentic Thai dishes that can be made with imported goods, or with your own local produce.

Opposite: *A floating market at Damnoen Saduak, southwest of Bangkok.*

STEP 3

STEP 3

STEP 4

STEP 5

STIR-FRIED GREENS

The water chestnuts in this recipe give a delicious crunch to the greens.
Several types of oriental greens can be successfully substituted
for the spinach.

SERVES 4

1 tbsp sunflower oil
1 garlic clove, halved
2 scallions, finely sliced
7½ ounce can water chestnuts, drained and
    finely sliced (optional)
1 pound spinach, any tough stalks
    removed
1 tsp sherry vinegar
1 tsp light soy sauce
pepper

1 Heat the oil in a wok or large, heavy skillet over a high heat.

2 Add the halved garlicclove, and cook, stirring, for 1 minute. If the garlic should brown, remove it immediately.

3 Add the sliced scallions and the water chestnuts, if using, and stir for 2–3 minutes. Add the spinach, and stir well.

4 Add the sherry vinegar, soy sauce, and a sprinkling of pepper. Cook, stirring, until the spinach is tender. Remove the garlic.

5 Use a slotted spoon in order to drain off the excess liquid, and serve immediately.

TIPS

These stir-fried greens are delicious served as an accompaniment to the Red Curry with Cashews (see page 36).
  Several types of oriental greens (for example, choi sam and pak choi) are widely available and any of these can be can be used instead of the spinach.

STEP 1

STEP 2

STEP 3

STEP 4

CAULIFLOWER WITH THAI SPINACH

This is a delicious way to cook cauliflower – even without the spinach!

SERVES 4

1³/₄ cups cauliflower florets
1 garlic clove
¹/₂ tsp turmeric
1 tbsp cilantro root or stem
1 tbsp sunflower oil
2 scallions, cut into 1-in. pieces
4 ounces Thai spinach, tough stalks
   removed, or oriental greens
1 tsp yellow mustard seeds

1 Blanch the cauliflower, and rinse in cold running water. Drain and set aside.

2 Grind the garlic, turmeric, and cilantro root or stem together in a pestle and mortar or spice grinder.

3 Heat the oil in a wok or large, heavy skillet. Add the scallions, and stir over a high heat for 2 minutes. Add the Thai spinach, or greens, and stir for 1 minute. Set aside.

4 Return the wok or skillet to the heat, and add the mustard seeds. Stir until they start to pop, then add the turmeric mixture and the cauliflower. Stir until all the cauliflower is coated.

5 Serve with the spinach or greens on a warmed serving plate.

SUBSTITUTES

Oriental greens are now available in many of the larger supermarkets; however, regular spinach or chard is equally good with the cauliflower.

MIXED VEGETABLES IN COCONUT MILK

This is a deliciously crunchy way to serve a mixture of vegetables.

STEP 1

SERVES 4–6

1 red chili, deseeded and chopped
1 tsp coriander seeds
1 tsp cumin seeds
2 garlic cloves, crushed
juice of 1 lime
1 cup coconut milk
2 cups bean-sprouts
2 cups shredded white cabbage
4 ounces snow peas, trimmed
1¼ cups thinly sliced carrots
1¼ cups cauliflower florets
3 tbsp peanut butter
grated or shaved coconut, to garnish

1 Grind together the chopped chili, coriander seeds, cumin seeds, and crushed garlic cloves in a pestle and mortar or food processor. Add the lime juice and mix well.

2 Put the spice and lime juice mixture into a medium saucepan, and heat gently until fragrant, about 1 minute. Add the coconut milk, and stir until just about to boil.

3 Meanwhile, mix all the vegetables together in a large bowl.

4 Stir the peanut butter into the coconut and spice mixture and combine with the vegetables. Sprinkle over slivers of grated or shaved coconut. Serve immediately.

STEP 2

STEP 3

TIPS

If you prefer, the cauliflower, carrots, and snow peas can be blanched before being mixed with the dressing, to give them less bite.

   This dish is ideal as a buffet dish as the quantity of dressing is quite sparse, and is only intended to coat, so you don't need too much of it to cover a large bowlful of vegetables.

STEP 4

STEP 2

STEP 3

STEP 3

STEP 4

CARROT & CILANTRO SALAD

This is a tangy, crunchy salad, which is popular with everyone. It makes an ideal accompaniment to Eggplant & Mushroom Satay with Peanut Sauce (see page 42).

SERVES 4

4 large carrots
2 celery stalks, cut into matchsticks
2 tbsp roughly chopped fresh cilantro

DRESSING:
1 tbsp sesame oil
1½ tbsp rice vinegar
½ tsp sugar
½ tsp salt

1 To create flower-shaped carrot slices, as shown, cut several grooves lengthwise along each carrot before slicing it.

2 Slice each carrot into very thin slices, using the slicing cutter of a grater.

3 Combine the carrot, celery, and cilantro in a bowl. Combine the dressing ingredients thoroughly.

4 Just before serving, toss the carrot mixture in the dressing, and transfer to a serving dish.

GARNISHES

You can make this attractive salad look even more appealing with the addition of a simple garnish. Cut very fine strips of carrot with a vegetable peeler and curl them into a spiral, or drop in iced water for a few minutes to make them curl up. Alternatively you could make very thin cuts through a chunk of celery from the top almost to the bottom, and leave in iced water until the fronds curl up.

SESAME OIL

Sesame oil is a very aromatic oil used in small quantities in a lot of oriental cooking, to impart a special flavor to salad dressings and sauces. If it is not available, you can substitute any high quality oil, though the dressing will not have the distinctive Thai flavor.

STEP 1

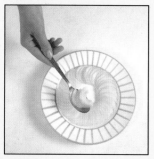

STEP 2

STEP 3

STEP 5

CUCUMBER SALAD

This is a very refreshing accompaniment to any main dish, and is an excellent "cooler" for curries. Alternatively, it can be served simply as a salad on a buffet.

SERVES 4

¹/₂ English cucumber
1 tbsp rice vinegar
2 tbsp sugar
2 tbsp hot water
¹/₂ tsp salt
1 small shallot, thinly sliced

1 Peel the cucumber, and halve lengthwise. Deseed it, using a teaspoon or a melon baller.

2 Slice the cucumber thinly, and arrange the cucumber slices on a serving plate.

3 To make the dressing, combine the vinegar, sugar, and salt in a bowl. Pour on the hot water and stir until the sugar has dissolved.

4 Pour the dressing over the cucumber.

5 Sprinkle the shallot slices over the cucumber. Chill the salad in the refrigerator before serving.

RICE VINEGAR

There are two kinds of rice vinegar, each of which is less acidic than Western vinegars. Red vinegar is made from fermented rice, and has a dark color and depth of flavor. White rice vinegar is distilled from rice wine and has a stronger flavor than red vinegar. Because of this distinctive but subtle flavor, white rice vinegar is preferred by many Western cooks. If it is unavailable, you can use white wine vinegar or cider vinegar.

CUCUMBERS

Some people dislike the bitter taste that cucumbers can have – I find that peeling off the skin and deseeding often eliminates this problem.

Using a melon baller is the neatest method of deseeding a cucumber, although a rounded teaspoon will do just as well instead.

STEP 1

STEP 2

STEP 3

STEP 4

GRAPEFRUIT AND COCONUT SALAD

This salad is deceptive – it is in fact quite filling, even though it looks very light.

SERVES 4

1 cup grated coconut
2 tsp light soy sauce
2 tbsp lime juice
2 tbsp water
2 tsp sunflower oil
1 garlic clove, halved
1 onion, finely chopped
2 large ruby grapefruit, peeled and
*   segmented*
1¹/₂ cups alfalfa sprouts

1 Toast the coconut in a dry skillet, stirring constantly, until golden-brown, about 3 minutes. Transfer to a bowl.

2 Add the light soy sauce, lime juice, and water.

3 Heat the oil in a saucepan, and fry the garlic and onion until soft. Stir into the coconut mixture. Remove the garlic with a spoon.

4 Divide the grapefruit segments between 4 plates. Sprinkle each with a quarter of the alfalfa sprouts, and then spoon over a quarter of the coconut mixture.

ALFALFA SPROUTS

Alfalfa sprouts can be bought in trays or packages from most supermarkets, but you can easily grow your own, if you like to have a constant and cheap supply.

Soak a couple of tablespoons of alfalfa seeds overnight in warm water. Drain the seeds and place them in a glass jar, or a sprouting tray if you have one. Cover the neck of the jar with a piece of cheesecloth or fine netting. Leave in a dark, warm place. Once a day, fill the jar with warm water, then turn it upside down and allow the water to drain out through the cheesecloth. After 3 or 4 days, the seeds will be ready to eat.

You can sprout almost any seeds and beans in this way, including mung beans, which turn into bean-sprouts, and are usually much crunchier than the store-bought variety.

STEP 1

STEP 2

STEP 3

STEP 5

CELERY & GREEN BELL PEPPER WITH SESAME DRESSING

A very elegant and light salad which will complement rice and noodle dishes beautifully.

SERVES 4

2 cups bean-sprouts
1½ tbsp chopped cilantro
3 tbsp fresh lime juice
½ tsp mild chili powder
1 tsp sugar
½ tsp salt
3 celery stalks, cut into 1-in. pieces
1 large green bell pepper, chopped
1 large green apple
2 tbsp sesame seeds to garnish

1 Rinse and drain the bean-sprouts. Pick them over and remove any that seem a little brown or limp – it is essential that they are fresh and crunchy for this recipe.

2 To make the dressing, combine the cilantro, lime juice, chili powder, sugar, and salt thoroughly.

3 In a large bowl, combine the celery, bell pepper, bean-sprouts, and apple.

4 To prepare the garnish, toast the sesame seeds in a dry skillet until they are just colored.

5 Stir the dressing into the mixed vegetables just before serving. Garnish with the toasted sesame seeds.

FRESH INGREDIENTS

Keeping each ingredient as fresh and crunchy as possible will make all the difference to the appearance and taste of this elegant salad. Choose the freshest, whitest bean-sprouts, and discard any limp or yellowed cilantro leaves.

APPLES

To prevent the apple slices from going brown, place in a little lemon juice and water as soon as you have cut them, and turn them in the juice to ensure they are fully covered.

CHAPTER FIVE

Buffet Dishes

Thai cuisine lends itself brilliantly to party food – it is always colorful, exquisitely presented, and made for sharing.

Any Thai meal eaten in an ordinary Thai home will be presented as three or four dishes or more, arranged around a central steaming hot bowl of fragrant rice. Each diner takes some rice and some of each dish in turn, all meant to be savored with the rice. However, a Thai meal eaten in a rather grander home or palace will be in the same format, but the dishes will be chosen from the slightly more elaborate "Royal Cuisine" which is the origin of the Little Golden Packages (see page 64) and the Fried Rice in Pineapple (see page 68).

It is in a "Royal" meal that one will see the most elaborate garnishes. With the aid of a very small, very sharp knife, and several years' experience, the royal vegetable carver will transform carrots, onions, apples, and chili into beautiful blossoms, birds, lilies, and fishes. You can emulate this with a simple scallion tassel or chili flowers to garnish a party buffet, and, with practise, carrot flowers or potato birds.

Opposite: *A banana seller in Chiang Mai.*

STEP 1

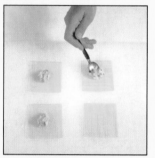

STEP 2

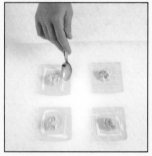

STEP 3

STEP 3

LITTLE GOLDEN PACKAGES

These little packages will draw admiring gasps from your guests, but they are fairly simple to prepare.

MAKES 30

1 garlic clove, crushed
1 tsp chopped cilantro root
1 tsp pepper
1 cup boiled mashed potato
1 cup water chestnuts, finely chopped
1 tsp grated gingerroot
2 tbsp ground roast peanuts
2 tsp light soy sauce
$^1/_2$ tsp salt
$^1/_2$ tsp sugar
30 wonton sheets, defrosted
1 tsp cornstarch, made into a paste with a
    little water
vegetable oil for deep-frying
fresh chives to garnish
sweet chili sauce, to serve

1 Combine all the ingredients thoroughly, except the wonton sheets, cornstarch, and oil.

2 Keeping the remainder of the wonton sheets covered, lay 4 sheets out on a counter. Put a teaspoonful of the mixture on each.

3 Make a line of the cornstarch paste around each sheet, about $^1/_2$ in. from the edge. Bring all four corners to the center and press together to form

little bags. Continue the process until all the wonton sheets are used.

4 Meanwhile, heat 2 inches of the oil in a deep saucepan until a light haze appears on top and lower the packages in, in batches of 3. Fry until golden brown, and remove with a slotted spoon, to drain on paper towels.

5 Tie a chive around the neck of each bag to garnish, and serve with a sweet chili sauce for dipping.

WONTON SHEETS

If wonton sheets are not available, use spring roll sheets or filo pastry, and cut the large squares down to about 4 inches square.

STEP 1

STEP 2

STEP 3

STEP 4

SON-IN-LAW EGGS

This recipe is supposedly so called because it is an easy dish for a son-in-law to cook to impress his new mother-in-law!

SERVES 4

6 eggs, hard-cooked and shelled
4 tbsp sunflower oil
1 onion, thinly sliced
2 fresh red chilies, deseeded and sliced
2 tbsp sugar
1 tbsp water
2 tsp tamarind pulp
1 tbsp liquid seasoning, such as
    Maggi

1 Prick the hard-cooked eggs 2 or 3 times with a toothpick.

2 Heat the oil in a wok or large, heavy skillet, and fry the eggs until crispy and golden. Remove and drain on paper towels.

3 Halve the eggs lengthwise, and put on a serving dish.

4 Reserve 1 tablespoonful of the oil, and pour off the rest. Then heat the tablespoonful in the wok or skillet. Cook the onion and chilies over a high heat until golden and slightly crisp. Drain on paper towels.

5 Combine the sugar, water, tamarind pulp, and liquid seasoning. Simmer for 5 minutes until thickened.

6 Pour the sauce over the eggs and spoon over the onion and chilies. Serve immediately with rice.

TAMARIND PULP

Tamarind pulp is commonly sold in oriental stores, and is quite sour. If it is not available, use twice the amount of lemon juice in its place.

PERFECT EGGS

When hard-cooking eggs, stir the water gently one way, then the other, and you will have beautifully centered yolks.

STEP 2

STEP 2

STEP 3

STEP 4

FRIED RICE IN PINEAPPLE

This looks very impressive on a party buffet, and has a mild, pleasant flavor, so everyone can sample it. However, if you simply want to serve it as a main course, quarter the pineapple, and carry on with the recipe.

SERVES 4–6

1 large pineapple
1 tbsp sunflower oil
1 garlic clove, crushed
1 small onion, diced
$^{1}/_{2}$ celery stalk, sliced
1 tsp coriander seeds, ground
1 tsp cumin seeds, ground
$1^{1}/_{2}$ cups sliced button mushrooms
$1^{1}/_{3}$ cups cooked rice
2 tbsp light soy sauce
$^{1}/_{2}$ tsp sugar
$^{1}/_{2}$ tsp salt
$^{1}/_{4}$ cup cashew nuts

TO GARNISH:
1 scallion, finely sliced
fresh cilantro leaves
fresh mint sprig

1 Halve the pineapple lengthwise, and cut out the flesh to make 2 boat-shaped shells. Cut the flesh into cubes, and reserve 1 cup to use in this recipe. (Any remaining pineapple cubes can be served separately.)

2 Heat the oil in a wok or large, heavy skillet. Cook the garlic, onion, and celery over a high heat, stirring constantly, for 2 minutes. Stir in the coriander and cumin seeds, and the mushrooms.

3 Add the pineapple cubes and cooked rice to the pan, and stir well. Stir in the soy sauce, sugar, salt, and cashew nuts.

4 Using 2 spoons, lift and stir the rice for about 4 minutes until it is thoroughly heated.

5 Spoon the rice mixture into the pineapple boats. Garnish with scallion slices, cilantro leaves, and the mint sprig.

PINEAPPLE

The remaining pineapple flesh can be combined with papaya and mango for an exotic fruit salad, which is delicious served in pineapple boats or a watermelon basket. For instructions on how to make a watermelon basket, see page 72.

SPRING ROLLS

The Thai spring rolls are not as heavy as the Chinese version and are ideal as canapés with drinks or as part of a finger buffet. The easiest way to break the rice vermicelli is to crush it in the packet before opening it to weigh it.

SERVES 6

2 tbsp all-purpose flour
²/₃ cup water
½ cup dried rice vermicelli, broken into small pieces
1 garlic clove, crushed
1 green bell pepper, deseeded and finely chopped
1 celery stalk, finely chopped
2 scallions, finely chopped
1¹/₃ cups finely sliced button mushrooms
2 tsp liquid seasoning, such as Maggi
½ tsp sugar
8 frozen spring roll sheets, 10 inches square, defrosted
oil for frying

SAUCE:
4 tbsp rice vinegar
4 tbsp sugar
½ tsp salt
1 small red chili, deseeded and finely chopped

1 Mix the flour and water together over a low heat, stirring constantly until thick and translucent. Pour into a saucer, and set aside.

2 Blanch the rice vermicelli in boiling water for 30 seconds. Stir and drain. Set aside.

3 Heat 1 tablespoon of the oil in a wok or large, heavy skillet over a high heat. Add the garlic, green bell pepper, celery, scallion, and button mushrooms. Stir until the vegetables are softened. Add the liquid seasoning and sugar. Remove from the heat, and transfer to paper towels to drain briefly. Stir into the rice vermicelli.

4 Cut the first spring roll sheet into 4 squares. Place about 2 tsp of the vermicelli mixture in the center of each square. Fold three corners inward like an envelope, and roll up to the fourth corner. Dab a little of the flour and water paste on this corner to seal. At this stage the spring rolls can be chilled or frozen for later use.

5 Heat the oil in a wok or deep-fat kettle until a light haze appears on top. Have ready a plate lined with paper towels. Deep-fry the spring rolls in batches until golden-brown. Drain well on the paper towels.

6 To make the sauce, boil all the ingredients together, stirring frequently until the sauce thickens, about 5 minutes. Pour into a small bowl or saucer. Serve with the spring rolls.

STEP 1

STEP 3

STEP 4

STEP 6

STEP 1

STEP 2

STEP 3

STEP 4

MANGO SALAD

A version of this popular salad is sold all over Thailand. It is an unusual combination, but works well as long as the mango is very unripe. Papaya can be used instead, if you prefer. The components of the salad can be prepared ahead, but should not be assembled until just before serving, so that the flavors remain distinct.

SERVES 4

1 lollo biondo, or any crunchy lettuce
¼ cup fresh cilantro leaves
1 large unripe mango, peeled and cut into
    long thin shreds
1 small red chili, deseeded and finely chopped
2 shallots, finely chopped
2 tbsp lemon juice
1 tbsp light soy sauce
6 roasted canned chestnuts, quartered

1 Line a serving plate or watermelon basket (see box, right) with the lettuce and cilantro.

2 Soak the mango briefly in cold water, in order to remove any syrup, while you prepare the dressing.

3 Combine the chili, shallots, lemon juice, and soy sauce.

4 Drain the mango, and combine with the chestnuts. Spoon onto the serving plate.

5 Pour over the dressing, and serve immediately.

HANDY HINT

This would look wonderful if served in a watermelon basket. To make a watermelon basket, stand a watermelon on one end on a level surface. Holding a knife level and in one place, turn the watermelon on its axis, so that the knife marks an even line all around the middle. Mark a 1 in. wide handle across the top and through the center stem, joining the middle line at either end. (If you prefer a zigzag finish, mark the shape to be cut at this point before any cuts are made, to insure even zigzags.)

Take a sharp knife and, following the marks made for the handle, make the first vertical cut. Then cut down the other side of the handle. Now follow the middle line, and make your straight or zigzag cut, taking care that the knife is always pointing toward the center of the watermelon, and is level with the counter, as this insures that when you reach the handle cuts, the cut-out piece of melon will pull away cleanly. Hollow out the flesh with a spoon, leaving a clean edge, and fill as required.

STEP 1

STEP 1

STEP 2

STEP 3

CORN PATTIES

These are a delicious addition to any party buffet, and very simple to prepare. Serve with a sweet chili sauce.

MAKES 12

11 ounce can sweetcorn, drained
1 onion, finely chopped
1 tsp curry powder
1 garlic clove, crushed
1 tsp ground coriander
2 scallions, chopped
3 tbsp all-purpose flour
$\frac{1}{2}$ tsp baking powder
salt
1 large egg
4 tbsp sunflower oil

1 Mash the drained sweetcorn lightly in a medium-sized bowl. Add all the remaining ingredients, except for the oil, one at a time, stirring after each addition.

2 Heat the oil in a skillet. Drop tablespoonfuls of the mixture carefully onto the hot oil, far enough apart for them not to run into each other as they cook.

3 Cook for 4–5 minutes, turning each patty once, until golden-brown and firm. Take care not to turn them too soon, or they will break up in the pan.

4 Remove from the pan with a slice, and drain on paper towels. Serve while still warm.

PRESENTATION

To make this dish more attractive, you can serve the patties on large leaves, like those shown. Be sure to cut the scallions on the slant, as shown, for a more elegant appearance.

TIME SAVER

The mixture can be made in advance and will keep in the refrigerator for up to 2 days.

THAI CUISINE

FLAVORINGS

It is the spices and flavorings that give Thai food its essential character, and a few of these are listed below – but do not be deterred, for you will be amazed at how few basic spices are needed to get you started in Thai cuisine. Many of these are now available in larger supermarkets and health-food stores, though you may occasionally have to hunt them out in greengrocers or oriental food stores. Alternatives are suggested wherever possible.

Chili

There are several kinds of chilies, the basic rule being the smaller they are, the hotter they are. Raw chilies can irritate the skin, so rub a little salt on your hands before and wash them immediately after handling the chilies. Do not touch your eyes or face until you have thoroughly washed the chili juices from your hands. I have tempered these recipes for Western tastes, but if you prefer a hotter bite, simply add more chilies.

Cilantro

This is an essential ingredient for Thai cooking. If the recipe requires root and stalk, do use this part of the plant, as it has a unique flavor. Fresh cilantro is usually available with its roots from markets and oriental stores, and you will find the leaves in larger supermarkets.

FOOD AND CULTURE IN THAILAND

Thailand lies in South-east Asia, and is a country where, as in much of the Far East, the 20th century lives comfortably side by side with ancient Thailand, rich in art and architecture, tradition, and culture.

Food and culture are inextricably bound in every part of the Thai daily routine. The country draws much of its wealth from the abundance of lush green countryside where the Thai farmers grow a huge array of natural produce, and this wide variety of fresh ingredients is the backbone of Thai cuisine.

The daily routine

The pleasure of coming to the table and eating is very important to the Thai people, and the way they go about their eating depends on their lifestyle, whether they be city or country workers and dwellers.

Before the first meal of the day the family will wait for the Buddhist monks to come to their gate or the riverside entrance to their home, or knock on the elevated door to collect their daily alms – a gift of food, usually part of the morning meal. Although the Buddhists will not kill animals to eat, they cannot refuse an offering of food, so this way they end up eating a certain amount of meat without compromising themselves.

Fast foods

From then until the evening meal, the average office worker will snack several times, choosing from the huge variety of roadside food stalls and more mobile street vendors, who will sell such things as noodle dishes in myriad forms. These dishes, something between a soup and a stew, are assembled swiftly and deftly before your eyes in a space the size of the wok and not much bigger, and into them will go the flavorings, the broth and the noodles, and it is up to the diners to indicate at the appropriate stage how much or little chili they would like. If they misjudge it, they can be sure of a fiery "kick-start" to the day! The Thai street vendors carry their wares suspended from either end of a bamboo pole balanced across one shoulder, the ingredients in one basket and the equipment in the other. They call out the dish of the day, and will stop to feed anyone who requires it.

Later on in the day when the morning rush is over, and the day is hotting up, everybody has to slow down a little, the stores take a lunch break, stallholders have a snooze, and the office workers go somewhere for lunch. As in any hot country, lunchtime is an extended affair, as it is too hot to move quickly and everyone waits until later in the afternoon, when the pace quickens again right into the evening.

For lunch the office worker may sit down at a roadside snack bar, or take a seat in one of the food markets, which are great fun for the gastronome. Surrounded by at least six or eight food stalls, you select a little of whatever you fancy, going back for more if you wish, and eating at long benches – a very sociable way to lunch. Of course, there are also Western-style restaurants in Bangkok, which are considered inexpensive by Western standards, but Thai people are not used to paying so much for their food.

The evening meal

The evening meal is the most sociable one in the Thai day, where allowance is usually made in case a couple of extra people join the family for dinner. Such unexpected guests are always welcome to drop by, and quite likely to. Even without these extra guests, the number of diners is usually quite large, as the extended family enjoys this meal together. It is prepared by the mother and daughters, while the men enjoy a pre-dinner drink of whisky, which has been very diluted, accompanied by some morsel picked up on the way home and shared. When the meal is ready, everyone is summoned to the table by the call of *kin khao* – eat rice.

The meal consists of an array of different dishes, usually three or four, all of which use a range of varied but complementary flavorings and spices. These dishes are in addition to the rice, the basis of the meal. If anything is drunk with the meal, it is usually water, or more diluted whisky, but most people will drink nothing. This might be because some people believe that if you drink water with the meal, the rice will swell in your stomach, and you will not be able to eat much – but I'm not sure how true that is!

Most Thai meals end with fresh fruit, unless sweets have been purchased from one of the stalls that sell an array of colorful, sickly-sweet blocks of confections. There is such a huge amount of fresh fruit available in Thailand that this is the usual choice. The housewife can select from a variety of mangoes and papayas, pineapples, oranges, the pungent durian fruit, pears, melons, plums, cherries and, of course, bananas.

For most, this evening meal will be the last of the day, although a hungry diner might take a late-night stroll through the town or village last thing in the evening, where he or she may be tempted again by the roadside vendors. These hard-working vendors seem never to sleep, and can still offer passing customers a range of snacks, such as spring rolls or fried rice or maybe some noodles before they at last retire for a few hours, and start their day of calling and frying, flavoring and serving all over again.

The vegetarian Thai

As in any hot country, Thailand has a history of vegetarian eating – an abundance of fresh fruit and vegetables, the absence of refrigeration, and the need for a quick sustaining meal adds up to a vegetarian culture. However, refrigeration is now easy, the majority of Thais are meat-eaters, and one has to go to the country to find the vegetarian cuisine.

The starting point is obviously the Buddhist monasteries, where they are forbidden to kill animals for meat, and do not eat meat except when given it in

Coconut and coconut milk
Fresh grated coconut is widely available, as is canned coconut milk, which can be used where fresh coconut milk is required. The Thais would produce coconut milk from fresh coconuts, but coconuts available elsewhere are usually not fresh enough for this purpose. Coconut milk is as rich as light cream and should be used accordingly.

Galangal
This is a root rather like ginger, but it has a more translucent skin and a pinkish tinge. It is peeled like ginger, but usually sliced, not slivered. It will freeze very well. It can be bought as a powder: if fresh galangal is unavailable, use 1 tsp powder to replace $1/2$ in.

Gingerroot
This is widely available, usually peeled, and then sliced, slivered, or diced. Do not use powdered ginger, as it is not from the same plant.

Kaffir lime leaf
These are dark green leaves, which are used in the same way as a bay leaf. They are available dried, but if bought fresh can be frozen very well. If they are not available, use 1 teaspoon grated lime rind in place of each lime leaf.

Lemon grass
Another staple of Thai cuisine. The stalks are quite tough, so

need fine chopping or slicing. They are available in bundles or in small packs from some supermarkets. They can be frozen very well. If unavailable, use 2 tsp grated lemon rind in place of each stalk.

Liquid seasoning
This is a little like soy sauce, and has a sharp, salty flavour.

Mushrooms
Oyster mushrooms are particularly suited to Thai cuisine, and dried Chinese mushrooms can be bought for a reasonable price in large bags in oriental stores. Do not use the stalks on these mushrooms as they are inedible. Field, straw, and crimini mushrooms are all equally tasty in Thai dishes.

Noodles
You will find two types of noodle in this book, rice noodles and egg noodles. Both are now available in larger supermarkets, but you will find a vast array available in oriental supermarkets, both flavored and plain.

Soy sauce
I have used the light soy sauce here, although normal soy sauce would be fine.

Spring roll sheets
These can be found in the freezer section of an oriental store, usually in 10 in. square sizes. Simply peel off what you

their daily alms. In the monasteries one will find a developed and refined vegetarian cuisine which uses fungi, pulses, and legumes as a source of protein. These monasteries are usually self-sufficient, and grow most of what they eat, so the monks have to be skilled farmers as well as skilled cooks to make the most of their harvest.

Vegetarian meals are often cooked as a matter of course in the country areas, where fresh produce is abundant and refrigeration more limited than in the cities. These meals are often not as refined as the monastery cuisine; simple dishes are constructed around a single vegetable, which is flavored strongly with spices and herbs. However, the meal is still based around rice, with three or four dishes – a dry curry, a salad, and a noodle soup – to eat with it, as is the custom countrywide.

In the cities there is a vegetarian movement which is modern, young, and new – in Bangkok one of the food markets is a dedicated Vegetarian Pavilion (this can be found at the Chatuchak Weekend Market). The vegetarian food that I sampled, in a vegetarian restaurant in Bangkok, was very different from anything I'd seen; not simply Thai dishes with the meat omitted, but dishes based on entirely different flavors, very fresh and clear, but very Thai.

I hope you will enjoy exploring Thai vegetarian cuisine with the aid of this book, and remember that these recipes are intended as a guide only. When you think you have the feel of Thai vegetarian cooking, and are acquainted

with the methods and techniques involved, do adapt and experiment. If certain fresh produce is not available, substitute something else, or fill your spring rolls or cucumber cups with your own mixture. Substitutes for the harder-to-get ingredients are explained in this section. The flavors will not be exactly authentic, but that isn't too important – you will still be able to produce delicious Thai dishes that are virtually as good as the real thing. Remember the Thai doctrine that life is meant to be fun or *sanuk*!

COOKING UTENSILS
A few words on kitchen utensils – any reasonably well-equipped Western kitchen will be fine for cooking Thai food, but if you intend to cook such food regularly, then I would suggest that the following purchases would prove most useful, and will be worth the investment:

Wok
Most Thai kitchens have 2 or 3 woks for versatility, but you will need only one. There are two types available: the traditional iron version and the modern nonstick version.

The traditional wok is extremely reasonable in price, but before it can be used, it must be seasoned. The retailer will give you full instructions, but this involves rubbing oil into the iron, heating it to a very high temperature for 20 minutes or so, then rubbing off the excess oil. For best results this should be repeated 2 or 3 times, and the coating will improve with use. The modern nonstick version is the one that I use, which gives perfectly good results. It is very simple to use, and is easy to lift. It does everything I need it to do, and then wipes clean afterward. However, if you purchase one of these, do remember not to use metal utensils as they will ruin the nonstick coating. Use wooden spoons or spatulas, or even wooden chopsticks, for an authentic touch. Many woks are sold complete with these utensils, including a handy rice paddle.

When you use your wok, make sure that you heat it to the right temperature before adding the oil, so that your vegetables will not stick to the side, or become soggy from being in the pan too long. If you need to lower the temperature temporarily, move it away from the heat source rather than reducing the heat. When stir-frying, keep all the ingredients on the move so that they do not have a chance to stick – this is especially important with rice and noodles, which is why I recommend using two spatulas for these ingredients. This also allows any excess water which would make the mixture soggy to evaporate.

Woks are not used just for stir-frying – I find my wok ideal for deep-frying, as the angle of the sides means that any moisture evaporates easily and quickly, and a crisp finish is easier to obtain. However, be extremely careful when moving the wok when it is full of hot oil, as its more rounded shape makes it less stable than a saucepan. It is also quite possible to make soup and steam vegetables in a wok, if you like – experiment to find out which piece of equipment gives you the best results.

Pestle and mortar

These are available in wood or stone. The stone mortar gives a finer grind than the wooden mortar, and for this reason I use a stone mortar and pestle. They are available in several sizes at any good cookware or oriental store, and are inexpensive. Some people prefer to use a large pestle, which exactly fits the shape of the mortar, as this helps to prevent stubborn peppercorns flying out of the mortar! A coffee grinder can be substituted, but will need a good wipe with a damp cloth afterward, as some Thai spices are quite pungent. A blender or food processor will grind coarsely, and although it is not so good for grinding small quantities, it can be used for this purpose.

Rice cooker

It is worth investing in a rice cooker only if you are seriously keen on oriental and Indian foods, and eat large quantities of rice. Having said that, most Asian homes have 2, maybe 3 rice cookers of different sizes, and would be lost without one.

A Western version of an oriental rice cooker is available, but in my opinion this is not worth using, although it is tempting to buy one, as it is inexpensive compared to the Asian (usually Japanese) version. I use the Japanese version, and would find the Western one very unsatisfactory now. The Japanese rice cooker has treble-skinned walls, a steam outlet and an airtight seal – you can put in any kind of rice, add the water, switch on, and leave it to cook. It is a Rolls-Royce of rice cookers, but at a price.

need and re-freeze the remainder. If they are not available, use filo pastry instead, and cut to size.

Star anise
This is a Chinese spice with a distinctive liquorice flavor. It is available in powdered form: use 2 tsp to replace 1 star anise.

Tamarind
This is available in pulp form, and to extract the water, place it in a strainer over a bowl, pour over a little hot water, and press the pulp through. It is quite sour; if it is not available, substitute twice the amount of lemon juice.

Tempeh
This is usually found in the freezer section of your local health food store or oriental store. Tempeh can also be bought marinated or smoked.

Tofu
This is widely available, often in a marinated form or smoked. Made from soy beans, it has only a bland flavor, but it absorbs every other flavor in the dish, and is very nutritious.

Wonton wrappers
These dumpling wrappers are made to the same recipe as egg noodles, and can be found in the freezer section of an oriental store. They are usually 4 inches square; simply defrost, peel off what you need, and refreeze the remainder.

INDEX